STAR WARS
EPISODES I, II & III

Easy Piano

STAR WARS
(Main Title)

Music by **JOHN WILLIAMS**
Arranged by Dan Coates

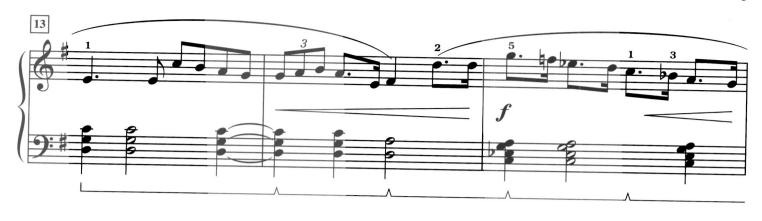

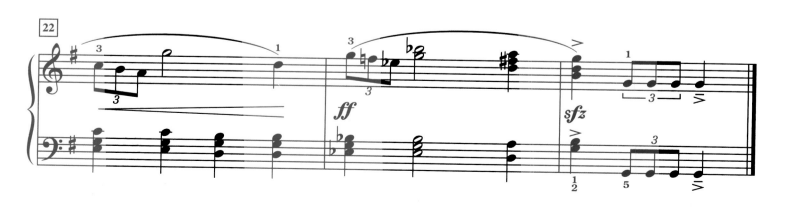

DUEL OF THE FATES

Music by **JOHN WILLIAMS**
Arranged by Dan Coates

AUGIE'S GREAT MUNICIPAL BAND

Music by **JOHN WILLIAMS**
Arranged by Dan Coates

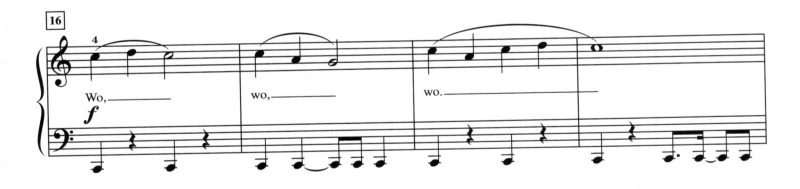

QUI-GON'S FUNERAL

Music by **JOHN WILLIAMS**
Arranged by Dan Coates

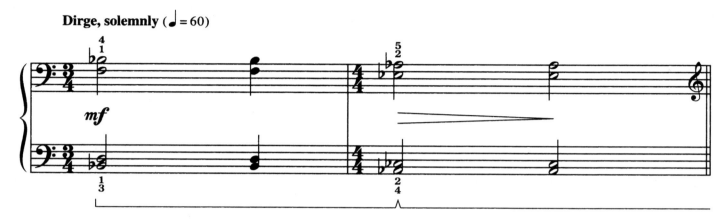

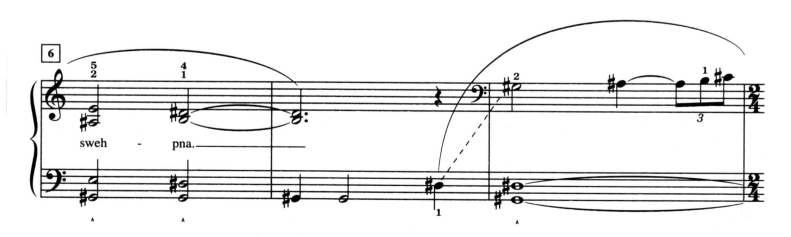

Ma - phu - rah sweh - pna go

rah - do - mah sweh - pna, moor - it - tioo,

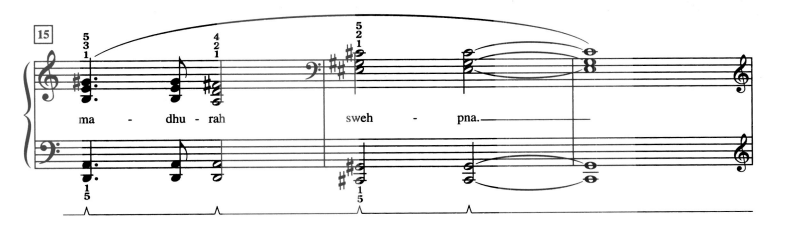

ma - dhu - rah sweh - pna.

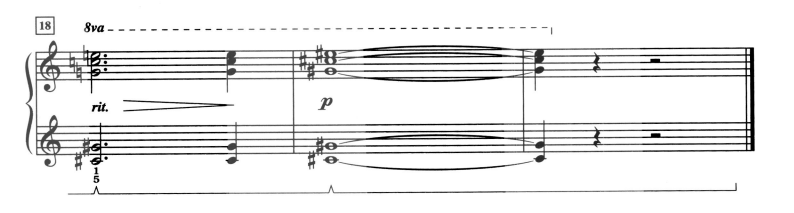

ACROSS THE STARS

Music by **JOHN WILLIAMS**
Arranged by Dan Coates

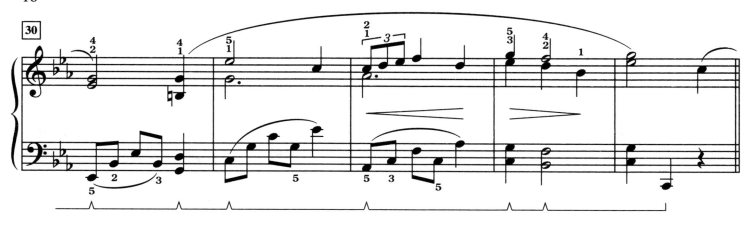

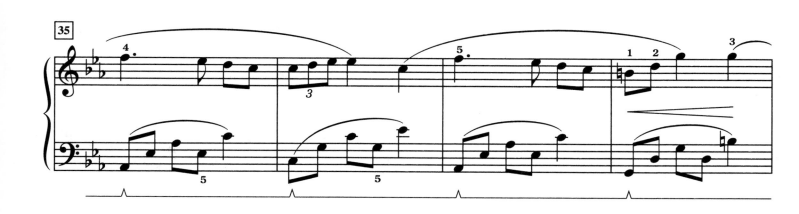

Appassionato

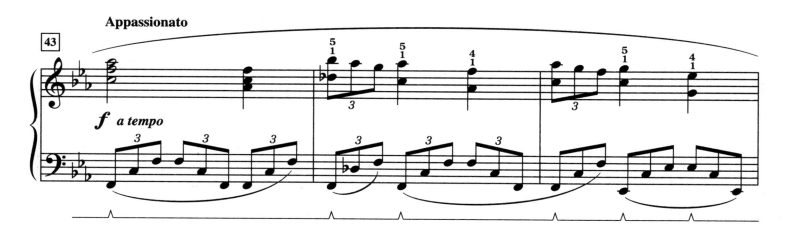

THE IMPERIAL MARCH
(Darth Vader's Theme)

Music by **JOHN WILLIAMS**
Arranged by Dan Coates

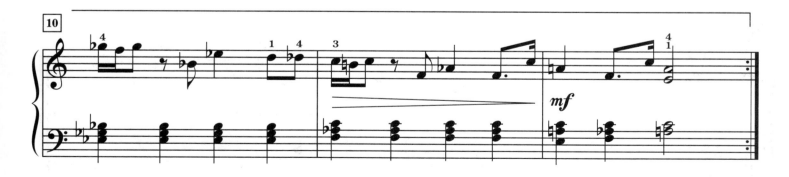

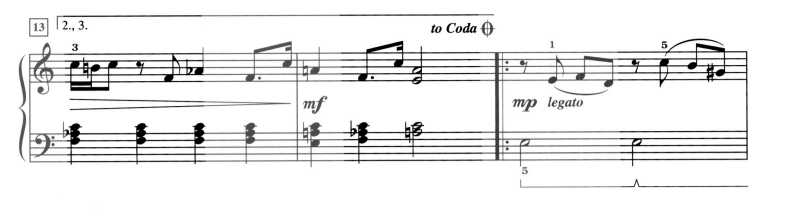

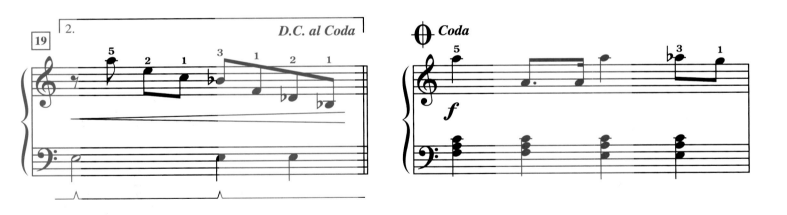

MAY THE FORCE BE WITH YOU

Music by **JOHN WILLIAMS**
Arranged by Dan Coates

THE MEADOW PICNIC

Music by **JOHN WILLIAMS**
Arranged by Dan Coates

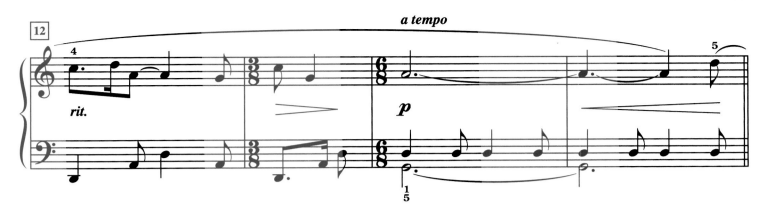

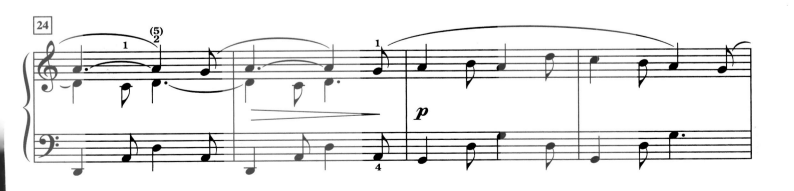

PRINCESS LEIA'S THEME

Music by **JOHN WILLIAMS**
Arranged by Dan Coates

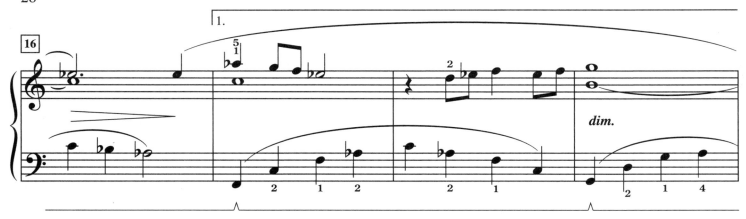

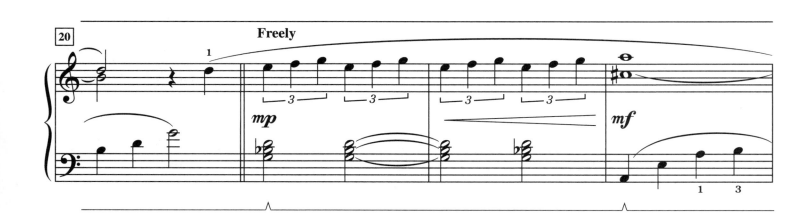

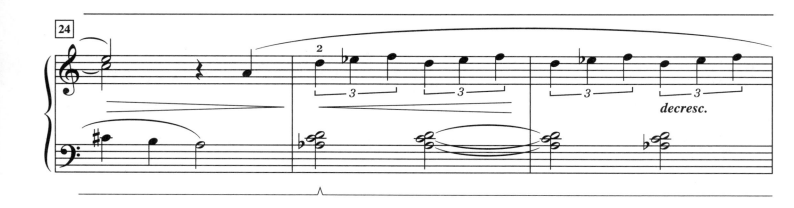

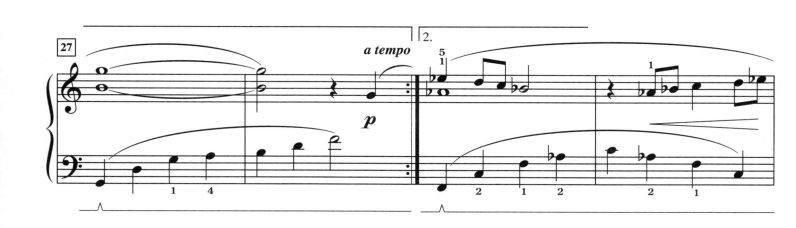

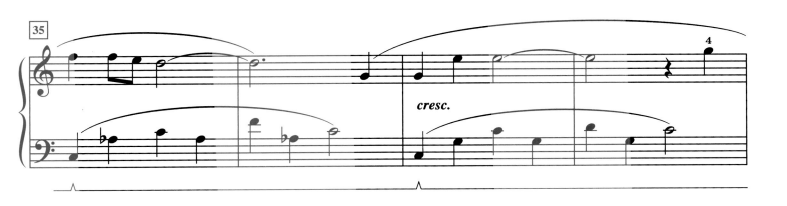

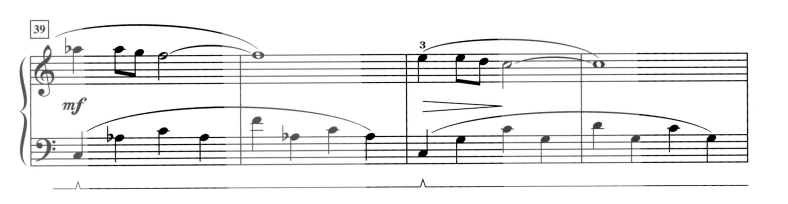

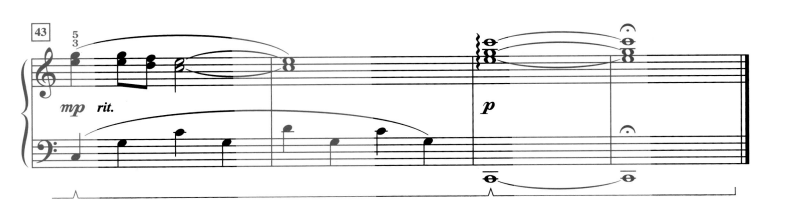

BATTLE OF THE HEROES

Music by **JOHN WILLIAMS**
Arranged by Dan Coates

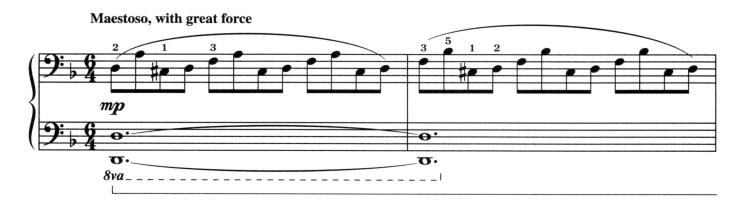

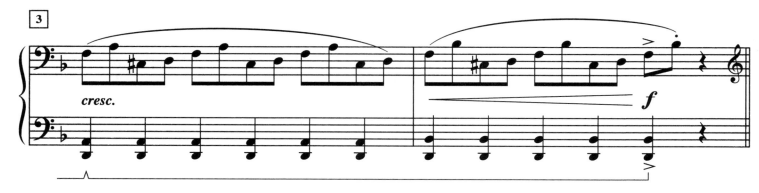

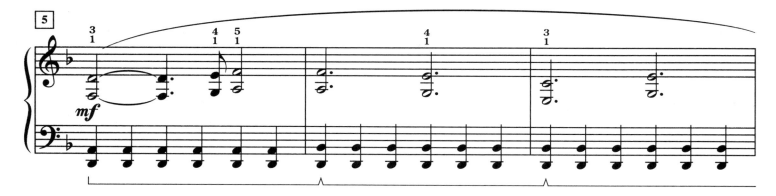

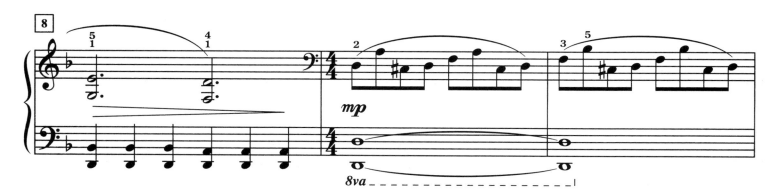

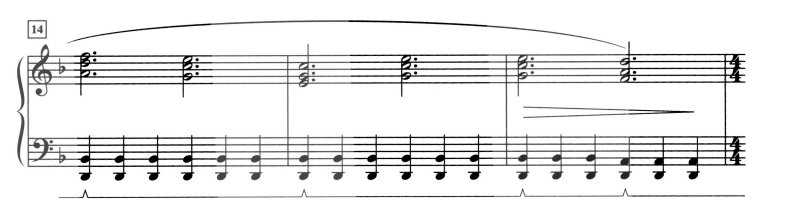

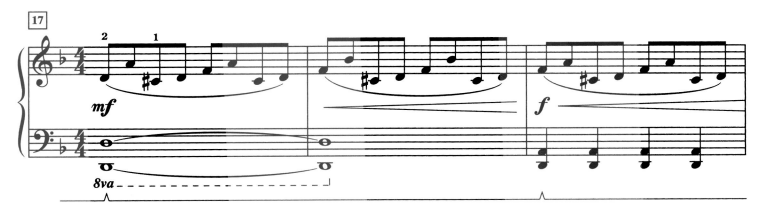

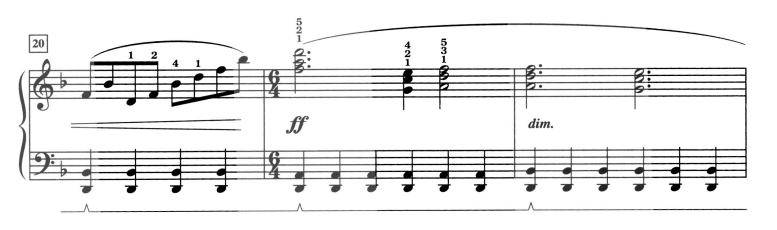

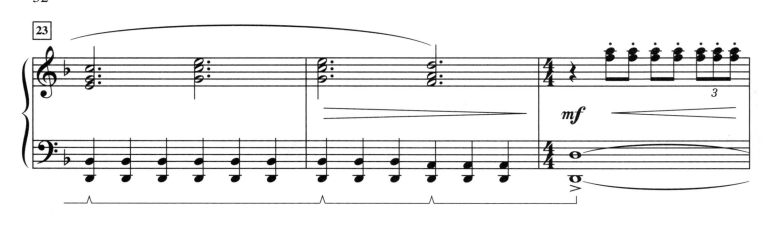

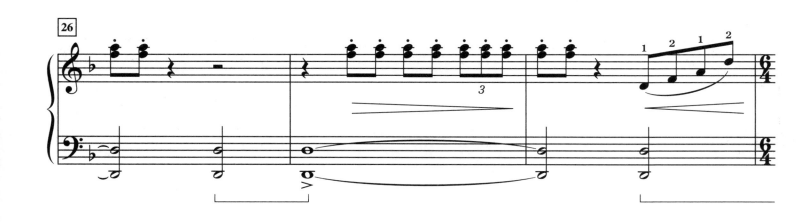

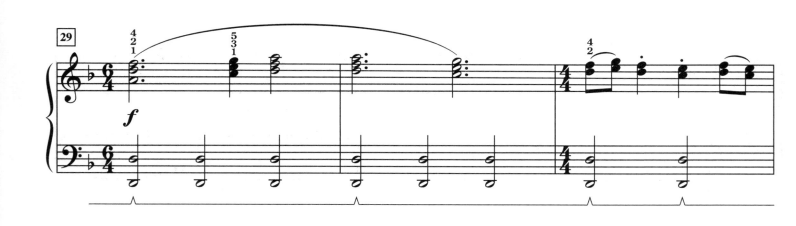

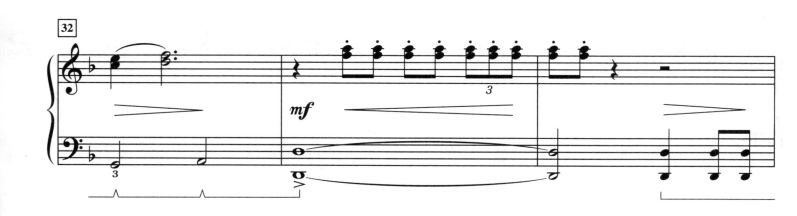

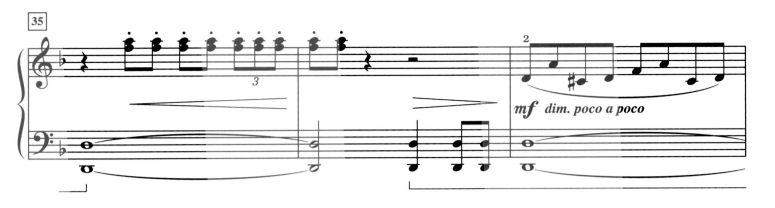

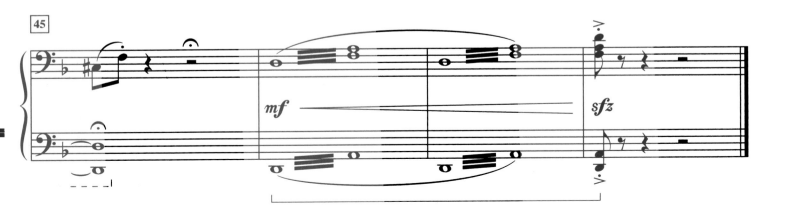

THE THRONE ROOM

Music by **JOHN WILLIAMS**
Arranged by Dan Coates

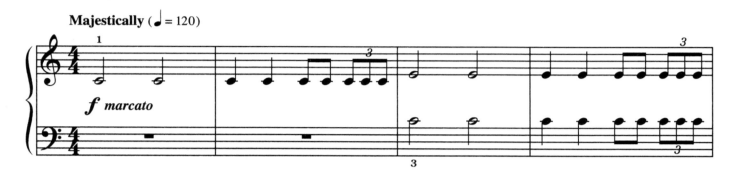

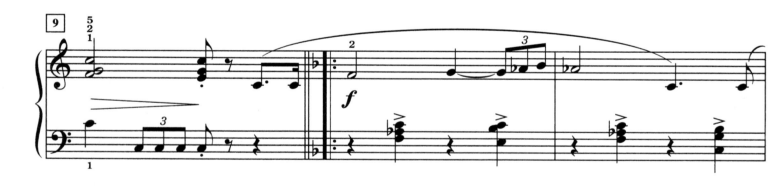

36